The sand the salt and the sea

Nicole Roache

BookLeaf Publishing

Presentation by *BookLeaf Publishing*

Web: www.bookleafpub.com

E-mail: info@bookleafpub.com

ISBN: 9789357448994

First edition 2021

DEDICATION

For my best boy and my best man.

ACKNOWLEDGEMENT

Thanks to Emma for the inspiration.

PREFACE

This collection brings together things I have thought about over the past month expressed through poetry. It seemed like a good idea at the time...

Advice for the living

Live as you love.
Taking care of what's precious.
But not being careful.
Live bravely.
Say the words.
Do the deeds.
Let your life be self-explanatory.
But don't be simple.
Have complex thoughts.
Ask all the questions.
Have deep conversations.
But don't get caught in the bull shit.

Annie

A little bundle of joy.
So wanted, so loved.
So like her dad, with golden curls.
A big voice.
Thoughts and expressions.
Knows her mind and speaks it well.
That sweet face.
Her smile shining bright.
Eyes dancing with intelligence.

At either end of the day

There is a special time at either end of the day.
A beginning, the orb breaches the horizon.
Shards of colour heralding the start.
A day full of promise.

Later, when all is quieting.
The great light begins its descent.
Dipping below the skyline.
The sky sings pink and orange in farewell.

Barney

Little google, who knows it all.
Such love in those dark eyes.
Donald Trump eyebrows and a batman mask.
Jumping from the couch and snapping at flies.
Cuddles and licks from a beautiful boy.
Who is our fur kid and so much more.
He finds you a stick and chases his ball
And has been called OCD and a bore.
But we love his quirks and personality.
His singing and refined taste.
When we're not home, we know you're just waiting.
For your humans, your loves and your mates.

Champagne

Heady bubbles
A dewy glow
Yeasty smell of toast and straw
Strawberries and citrus
A cool trail of fizz
Warms the insides
Widens the smile
Raises the voice

A toast!

Dad

A big hulking man
Full of songs and stories.
A worker, a player.

Physically strong
But soft on the inside
He loved his family.

A risk taker
Pushed to the limits
Made few mistakes.

Led from the front
Not on board?
His way or the highway.

A sweet tooth
A drinker
Social to the end.

A great father and friend
Gone too soon
Miss you Dad.

Dog day afternoon

An afternoon of boundless joy,
Is every day for this good boy.
Loving you with every part,
He makes wiggling and wagging quite the art.
A day of runs, of licks and pats,
Of friends, and wrestles, treats and snacks,
A cuddle first and then a snooze.
I'd like to walk a mile in those shoes.
They must have been wrong in that old show,
Afternoons like this are the best, I know.
It's clear that a dog day afternoon is definitely
not,
Boring and lifeless, though it might be hot…
Everyday should be a dog day afternoon!

Heaven Holes

Some days when you look into the sky
There is a sign shining from above
The clouds just break and the sun peeps through
A sign of heavenly love.

My mum went first, many years ago
My dad just two years past
So, when I see two beams poke through
I know they're on the task.

In early days Dad's rays were weak
With mum's so strong and true
But now they both can surely speak
Those beams say we love you.

I'm not

I am many things.
A sister, lover, friend and aunt.
But I am not a mother.

I always thought I would be,
A couple of kids, a picket fence, all that is
expected.
But I am not a mother.

I lacked ambition.
Waiting for a man and child.
But I am not a mother.

I feel different.
Conversations I can’t have.
Because I am not a mother.

I see families.
I think I would be good at that.
But I am not a mother.

I imagine my child.
The love I would have.
But I am not a mother.

I have tried.
To be other things, like a step-mother.
But I am not a mother.

I will die.
I won't have a legacy.
Because I am not a mother.

Lasts

A moment to treasure.
A story to share.
A truce to hold.
Or a grudge to bear.
A last is final.
It signals an end.
A change, a beginning
A bridge to mend.
A last is a gift.
So, keep them all near.
And never forget,
You have nothing to fear.

Little parachutes

I dropped my mask the other day
It fluttered to the ground,
Just like a little parachute.
All it needed was a man.

It made me contemplate the mask dilemma
I hate wearing them, but I know it's right
Just like I'd hate to need a parachute
To evacuate a plane mid-flight.

For now, our little parachutes
Are keeping germs away
Yes, they give us acne and sweaty face
Beats COVID any day.

Love

One day the merry-go-round stops.
You look at each other,
And make a silent pact.
You agree to compromise
To accept each other's faults
To work on this thing together.
That's love.
Making it work when it's hard.
Being kind when you want to scream.
Being present when you can't be bothered.
That's love.
The intimacy of a hug or a peck on the forehead.
The love you x text for no reason.
The I'm sorry text, for so many reasons.
That's love.
Being swept off your feet.
Fancy dates, exaggerated stories.
Stripping each other and shagging like rabbits.
That's not love.
Love is no matter what, no matter how.
It's forever.

Mum

It's been so long since I've seen you
I fear that the memories may fade
But I remember your laugh.
We talk speak of you often
Sharing stories
I can still hear your voice.
When I am doing things
When I hear things I say
I feel a lot like you.
In Sarah, in Sam, in Annie and even Maggie,
somehow
You are still so present
Your legacy lives in us.
I love you
I miss you
I remember you every day.

Open Water

Stroke.
Pull.
Kick.
Breathe.
Look up.
Breathe.
Keep rolling those arms.
Breathe.
Don't forget to kick.
Breathe.
Stretch your arms further.
Breathe.
Kick harder.
Breathe.
It's not a shark.
Breathe…

People

Some I love.
Others I don’t.
It’s simple.
Life is more complicated with them.
It is emptier without them.
They annoy you.
They inspire you.
They hurt you.
They love you.
Some of them do nothing.
I have a love hate relationship with people.

Skiing

Edges bite into the white.
Gripping but not slowing.
A feeling of control as you swoop into the turn.
Then the other way, a moment between turns
when you are careering straight.
True freedom. Quiet but for the planks on the
snow-covered ground.
The oof of a snowboarder falling somewhere.
Hopefully not in your line.
Clean air rushing past.
Eyes streaming from the cold behind goggles.
Burning quads make you forget the sub-zero
temperature.
Then suddenly you're at the lift.

Tea

There is nothing like a steaming mug in your hand.
Inspiring conversations or silence.
A moment for you.
Quenching your thirst and stilling your soul.
Breathe.
Watch the steam rise.
Warm your cold fingers.
Let the clarity settle.

Walks

With friends
And dogs
On beaches
And paths
To waterfalls
Down the street
In shoes
Bare feet
On grass
And sand
With purpose
For fun
To get somewhere
To take a moment
Walks.

Waterfall

Thundering water.
Air laden with tiny droplets.
A cool mist.
Trees, rocks and ferns.
A place of peace, yet never silent.
Cleansing, cold and deep.
A meandering creek then a drop creates this wonder.

Waves

The water surges
Peaking on the sand bar
Teetering until it gives in to gravity
Tumbling onto the surface, and below
Dissipating, in a haze of sand and foam
Stilling, the ocean returns to blue
And repeat

Why?

Do you have children?
No.
Why?

Did you choose not to have them?
Did your body let you down?
Didn't you meet anyone?
Subtext… what's wrong with you?

Oh.
You would have made a wonderful mum.
You'll regret it one day.
You just don't know love until you have a child.
Subtext… I'm judging you.

I know.
I know all of those things.
It wasn't my choice.
It was a combination of things mostly outside my control.
Subtext… I'm sorry.

Apologies.
For my life.
For being a lifeless hull.

For not meeting your expectations.
Subtext… I'm worthless.

www.ingramcontent.com/pod-product-compliance
Lightning Source LLC
Chambersburg PA
CBHW051759130826
49812CB00033B/1203
9789357448994